D0983516

Some Other Books by Ruth Brindze

Investing Money: The Facts about Stocks and Bonds
The Rise and Fall of the Seas: The Story of the Tides
The Sea: The Story of the Rich Underwater World

HURRICANES

Aircraft photograph of the eye of Hurricane Gracie,
September 28, 1959.   U.S. Navy Photograph

HURRICANES

Monster Storms from the Sea

RUTH BRINDZE

Illustrated with photographs

A Margaret K. McElderry Book

ATHENEUM 1973 *NEW YORK*

Front cover photograph courtesy of Aetna Life &
Casualty; back cover photograph courtesy of NOAA.

Published simultaneously in Canada by McClelland & Stewart, Ltd.
Manufactured in the United States of America
by Halliday Lithograph Corporation
West Hanover, Massachusetts
Designed by Nancy Gruber
First Edition

CONTENTS

1

When Great Hurricane Camille Hit the Gulf Coast

The first report about Great Hurricane Camille, the most intense storm ever to strike the United States, was issued at 1 P.M. on Thursday, August 14, 1969. In its Advisory No. 1 on Camille, the National Hurricane Center in Miami, Florida announced that a hurricane hunting plane, reconnoitering in the Caribbean, had flown into the storm 480 miles south of Miami. Camille had been born near the African coast, and before she was actually seen, her movement across the Atlantic had been tracked from weather satellite pictures. While the hurricane hunters were in the storm it intensified.

The National Hurricane Center said that Camille was moving toward the west tip of Cuba. No prediction was made as to the storm's path after it hit Cuba, but people living in southern Florida were told to be prepared to take rapid protective action. Florida has been lashed by more full hurricanes than any other section of the United States and Floridians who had lived through other hurricanes worried about Camille.

Advisory No. 2, issued by the National Hurricane Center at

6 P.M. Thursday evening, stated that Camille posed a threat to Florida and also to the east central section of the Gulf of Mexico. Ships traveling in areas that might be affected by the storm were urged to listen to broadcasts about Camille's development and movement. When a captain knows the path on which a storm is moving he can, by correct maneuvering, escape its full fury.

Throughout the night, advisories and bulletins were issued by the National Hurricane Center at three-hour intervals and were immediately broadcast. When Camille was nearing the United States' coast, official reports were given more frequently. Some were based on facts gathered by hurricane hunting planes and others on radar observations.

If a fleet of enemy bombers had been approaching, the situation could not have been more tense. Where would Camille make her landfall? When? Making such predictions is difficult because hurricanes frequently change course; they may swerve to the right or to the left and the speed at which they travel also varies.

On Friday, August 15, Camille grew in strength. The wind was estimated to be blowing at more than 115 miles per hour around the center of the hurricane. For 150 miles ahead of the storm the sea was whipped by gale winds. The Hurricane Center ordered gale warnings for the southern tip of Florida.

The midnight advisory on Friday said, "Camille a dangerous hurricane . . . entering the east portion of the Gulf of Mexico . . . poses a great threat to the United States mainland. . . . Camille is moving on a north northwesterly course at 10 mph . . . a little faster than earlier today."

By Saturday morning hurricane warnings were issued for the northwest coast of Florida. The hurricane warning signal, two

Gale Warning Storm Warning Hurricane Warning

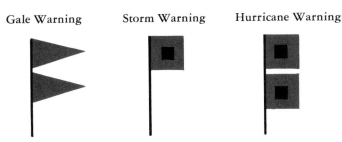

The flags used to show the predicted force of high winds. Two red pennants are hoisted one above the other for gales (winds of 39 to 54 mph). For storms (winds of 55 to 73 mph), the signal is a single square red flag with a black square in the center. For hurricanes (winds of 74 mph and over) two square red-and-black flags are displayed. U.S. Navy Photograph

red flags with black squares in the center, was hoisted at 11 A.M. A hurricane "warning" is an alert to prepare immediately for emergency conditions. At that time it was believed that Camille would make her landfall in Florida.

On Saturday afternoon the storm turned more to the west and a hurricane "watch" was announced for the Gulf of Mexico coast as far west as Biloxi, Mississippi. The term "watch" means that hurricane conditions are a real possibility but that the danger is not immediate.

Late Saturday afternoon, August 16, officials of Plaquemine Parish, low land near the mouth of the Mississippi River, decided that the area should be evacuated. If the storm tide rose to the predicted height of 15 feet (actually the rise was higher) most of the parish would be submerged.

Residents were urged to leave their homes while escape was possible. Civil defense officials broadcast appeals to evacuate and to make sure that everyone was warned; volunteers went from house to house urging people to go to hurricane shelters. Of the 20,000 people who lived in the parish, all but about 5 percent left their homes.

Many radio stations in the threatened area that normally sign off at midnight remained on the air to broadcast Camille's movements. During the intervals between the issuance of updated reports by the Hurricane Center, the most recent one was broadcast over and over again. There were also accounts of how other hurricanes had acted and since there was no prearranged program, some time was filled by playing music. Although few listeners were entertained by the music, it indicated that the

Hurricane warning flags flying near the waterfront of an area to which a hurricane poses a threat.   Ætna Life & Casualty

station was operating and would give the latest news of Camille.

The bulletin broadcast at 3 A.M. on Sunday morning, stated that Camille had been located by a hurricane hunting plane 260 miles south of Pensacola, Florida and that the outer fringes of the storm were coming within range of the New Orleans, Louisiana, and Apalachicola, Florida radar. Highest winds around the storm's center were estimated to be 160 miles an hour.

The 5 A.M. bulletin gave even worse news. Hurricane warnings had been extended as far west as Biloxi, Mississippi, and it was predicted that hurricane-force winds would hit in the afternoon or evening from Biloxi to northwest Florida.

At 7 A.M. it was announced that "Preparations against this dangerous hurricane should be completed as early as possible today in the area of hurricane warnings and persons in the area of hurricane watch should be prepared to take quick action if it becomes necessary to extend hurricane warning to the New Orleans–Grand Isle area."

While Camille churned toward the Gulf Coast, plans were developed by local officials and national organizations for coping with the storm. The disaster section of the American Red Cross arranged for shelter and food for thousands of expected storm refugees. State highway patrols established procedures for preventing traffic jams on roads that people, attempting to escape from the storm, would travel. Nearly 100,000 people fled inland from the coasts of Louisiana, Mississippi and Alabama.

The Gulf of Mexico is an important fishing area and is especially well known as a source of shrimp. Shrimp fishermen ordinarily moor their boats near their homes but such anchorages, although convenient, usually do not provide protection against the winds and waves of great storms. Every experienced fisherman knows a spot up a river or creek where a boat has the best chance of riding out a hurricane and, as Camille continued toward the Gulf Coast, fishing boats were moved to "hurricane holes."

Captains and crews of oceangoing ships loading or unloading cargoes in Gulf ports, stopped all regular work to concentrate on safeguarding their vessels. Anchors weighing hundreds of pounds were put out and shore lines, used to tie vessels to piers, were doubled and tripled. (Despite everything that was done to insure the ships' safety, many were wrecked. Some sank and others were hurled on the shore.)

Undersea oil mining is a major industry in the Gulf of Mexico. Mining equipment and living quarters for the miners are on large platforms standing on high legs driven into the sea bottom. Although designed to be "hurricane proof," many offshore oil production platforms have been torn apart by hurricanes. At mining company offices ashore, each new position given by weather forecasters for Camille was mapped. Depending on which way the storm turned, some mining sites would be in greater peril than others.

It is costly to shut down a mining operation, but most companies decided that Camille posed too great a threat to leave their men on platforms in the Gulf of Mexico. The men were brought ashore by helicopters and boats. The precaution proved to be wise; Camille wrecked three large platforms and partially destroyed more than fifteen others. The damage to the platforms amounted to more than $100 million.

By noon on Sunday it was dark as night in the city of Gulfport, Mississippi. Heavy rain fell and black clouds raced across the sky. The hurricane news was frightening. At 5 P.M. Camille was reported to be lashing the mouth of the Mississippi River.

One of the oil production platforms in the Gulf of Mexico wrecked by Camille. The damage to platforms and the equipment on them exceeded $100 million.   Chevron Oil Co.

At 7 P.M. the announcer said the center of the hurricane was moving toward Gulfport.

One man who lived in Gulfport had decided, after careful consideration, to ride out Camille in his own home. It was well built, was not near the waterfront and had withstood other hurricanes. In addition to his wife and seven children, the homeowner's father, mother, a friend, and a neighbor with her two children were in the house.

While they prepared for the storm, radios were kept tuned to news of Camille. All but the youngest children helped with the preparations. Since hurricanes often cause the contamination of the water supply, the bathtub was carefully cleaned and then filled with water that during, and after, the storm could be used for drinking. Jugs and pots were also filled with drinking water. Flashlights were placed in easy-to-find positions, and a battery-powered radio was brought into the living room for use if the storm knocked out the city's electric system. Porch furniture, bicycles, garbage cans, and other things normally left outside were carried indoors. A metal garbage can, propelled by hurricane force wind, can shatter a wall.

Even before the screaming wind reached maximum velocity the house shook and creaked. Rain, driven horizontally by the wind, bombarded the house and seeped through its thick walls. Attempts to mop up the water were given up when the front door blew away and rain flooded in. Then chunks of the ceiling began to fall. The noise of the wind sounded as if low flying planes were over the house.

When hurricane winds strike a building and pass over and around it, they exert both positive and negative forces. On the side of the building that the winds strike it pushes in, and on the opposite side it sucks out. The total of these two forces may be almost twice that of the winds' direct pressure. And that pressure alone is tremendous. Winds blowing at 200 miles an hour exert more than a ton of pressure on each ten square feet of the windward side of the building. An opening on that side adds to the winds' destructive power by increasing the positive pressure within the building. After the front door of the Gulfport house was blown off, the house shifted from its foundation.

Another mighty gust of wind tore the roof from the building. Hurricane winds passing over a building have the same effect as wind currents on the top surface of an airplane's wings. For an airplane, the wind currents contribute most of the lift; on a house, the suction of hurricane winds may lift off the roof.

When Great Hurricane Camille took off the roof of the Gulfport house the people inside were huddled in a small second floor room where they had taken refuge after the first floor was flooded. After two walls of the room collapsed, the father held

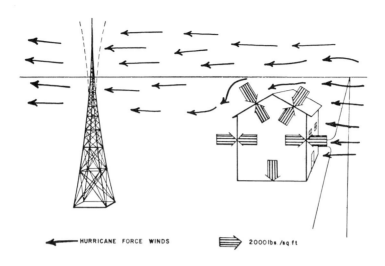

HURRICANE FORCE WINDS   2000 lbs /sq ft

Hurricane winds passing over and around a building develop both positive and negative forces. The positive forces are those pushing in; the negative forces are those pulling out. NOAA National Hurricane Research Laboratory Miami, Fla.

a mattress over the children to protect them from the rain and wind. When the floor began to sag, the father shouted directions for saving the children if the floor continued to give way. Almost miraculously the floor did not cave in.

Sometime after midnight the worst of the storm was over for Gulfport. The wind still howled but there were longer intervals between hard gusts. Gradually their force diminished; the people in the "safe" house had survived.

Not everyone was as lucky. In the debris of one luxury beach front apartment house, the bodies of twelve people who had gathered for a "hurricane party" were found. In addition to the 137 killed, more than 500 people were injured on the Gulf Coast.

Evacuation saved many lives that might have been lost when Camille turned buildings into rubble and the water rose over the

Camille wrenched this house from its foundation and left the building in a litter of wreckage.   American Red Cross photo by Ted Carland

rubble. One town in Plaquemine Parish, Louisiana was covered by 14 feet of water when a levee on the Mississippi River disintegrated.

Some people who remained in their homes instead of going to buildings designated as hurricane stations lived through hours of unimaginable terror. One elderly woman who lived alone was thrown out of her house when it was wrenched from its foundation. The woman landed in a large bush and clung to it until the storm abated. Fortunately the bush was on a little hill and there were no trees nearby. Trees are a hazard during a hurricane. When wind blows at 60 to 70 miles an hour, it rips off large branches and hurls them great distances, and when wind reaches 80 miles an hour big trees are uprooted and crash to the ground. Camille's winds gusted to more than 200 miles an hour.

Hurricane waves, racing inshore, gobble up miles of beaches

and the houses built upon them. A cubic yard of water weighs about three-fourths of a ton and a wave traveling at only 20 miles an hour has a battering force of more than 800 pounds per square foot. During severe hurricanes, waves may move at speeds as high as 50 or 60 miles an hour. The destructive power of the waves is increased by the tree trunks, parts of houses and other debris that they carry in and drive through whatever is in their path. Before the storm struck, there were one hundred fourteen elaborate residences in the beach-front area of Gulfport; after the storm there were only six that had escaped major damage. Nine had totally disappeared.

On Monday morning the sun shone in a blue sky. But for 55 miles along the coast there was rubble where houses had stood

A 10-foot long board was driven by the wind into the trunk of a royal palm tree. NOAA

An automobile squashed between two uprooted trees. In the fore-ground is a record player that was sucked out of a demolished house.

the night before. When a survey of the area was completed the figures showed that 5,579 homes had been destroyed, 12,491 had sustained major damage and another 25,090 had minor damage. Business buildings destroyed or with major damage numbered 726. At one military base with 150 large structures, about a third were damaged. Storm damage at other government bases was also great.

The storm left many grotesque sights. The wreckage of a large motel was buried under tons of fish fertilizer blown from a plant more than half a mile away. Thousands of large rolls of wrapping paper were strewn on the ground near a paper manu-facturing plant. An automobile stood on its front wheels with its back wheels balanced on a tree trunk. A boat had been blown halfway through a house and another boat was in a parking lot about three blocks from the beach. Many oceangoing ships weighing thousands of tons had been tossed up on land. As one man said, "The mind cannot accept what the eyes report."

The first task was to search for people buried alive in the rubble and to remove the bodies of the dead. Highways were blocked by blown-down trees, telephone and light poles. Trains could not run because tracks and bridges had been destroyed.

Planes brought in medical supplies, doctors, nurses and other workers needed to cope with the disaster situation.

The staff of the National Weather Service's radar station at Boothville, Louisiana, 60 miles southeast of New Orleans, was rescued on Monday afternoon by an Army "duck," a vehicle that can travel on land or water. The weather station had been built on ten-and-a-half-foot stilts to protect the structure from being flooded by storm tides, but the architects had not envisioned the height to which the sea rose during Great Hurricane Camille. On the first floor of the weather station the water was nearly five feet deep. The weathermen were safe enough on the second floor of the station but they were marooned there for nearly twenty-four hours. The station's costly scientific instruments that could not be carried to the second floor were ruined.

Most hurricanes weaken and die when they move inland but Camille was no ordinary storm. While traveling north over Tennessee and Kentucky, Camille dropped a moderate amount of rain that was welcome because there had been none for a long time. But when Camille crossed the mountains of West Virginia late Tuesday night, August 19, the rainfall was so heavy that in a few hours some areas were deluged by as much as 31 inches of rain. Scientists say that rain of this magnitude occurs, on an average, only once in a thousand years.

The water cascading down the mountains caused landslides that buried everything in their paths. Rivers, swollen by the rain, rose above their banks. The first flooding occurred during the night when people were asleep. Deaths resulting from floods totaled 155.

After moving three days overland, from August 17 to August 20, Camille headed back to sea near Norfolk, Virginia. The overland traveling had weakened her but Camille's winds were still 65 to 70 miles an hour. Camille lived on until August 22. By that date the remnants of the hurricane were 175 miles southeast of Cape Race, Newfoundland.

After the storm the Gulf Coast looked as though it had been heavily bombed. In the following three months more than 1,500,000 tons of debris was cleared in Mississippi and Louisiana. The repair and reconstruction of roads and bridges were given

Cartons of drinking water were distributed at Red Cross head-quarters in Gulfport. Camille's victims were also provided with food and clothing.   American Red Cross photo by Ted Carland

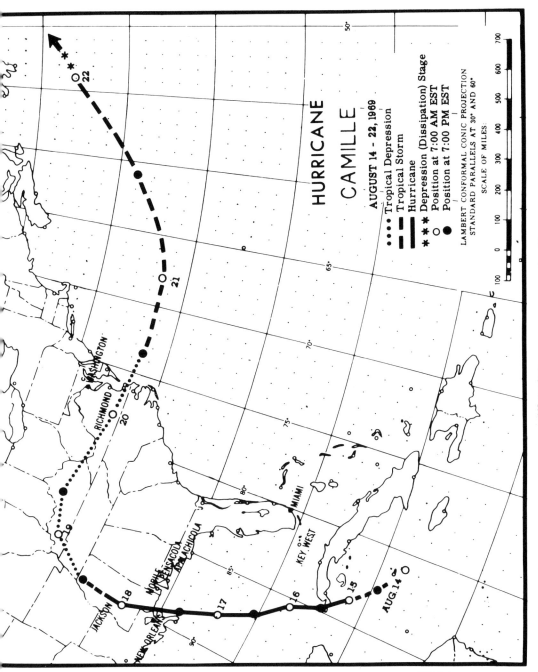

HURRICANE
CAMILLE
AUGUST 14 - 22, 1969

· · · · Tropical Depression
― ― ― Tropical Storm
━━━ Hurricane
* * * Depression (Dissipation) Stage
○ Position at 7:00 AM EST
● Position at 7:00 PM EST

LAMBERT CONFORMAL CONIC PROJECTION
STANDARD PARALLELS AT 30° AND 60°

SCALE OF MILES:

100   0   100   200   300   400   500   600   700

NOAA

Three large freighters, each weighing thousands of tons were driven ashore by the high winds and waves. Some smaller boats were blown farther inshore and tossed on houses.   NOAA

priority. Until roads were made usable there could be no semblance of normal life. The federal and state governments spent many millions to repair the damage done by Camille and thousands of people were forced to borrow money to rebuild their homes. The people who lived through Camille will never forget her.

Now that hurricanes are tracked and people in threatened areas are alerted, the deaths caused by the great storms have been sharply reduced. In contrast to the 137 men, women and children who lost their lives on the Gulf Coast during Camille, 6,000 people died, mostly by drowning, when a hurricane roared into Galveston, Texas, in 1900. Then there were no advance warnings. However, property damage caused by hurricanes is increasing. Camille caused damage officially fixed at $1,420,700,000, an amount that exceeded the loss from any previous hurricane. In 1972, the estimated loss from Agnes was more than $3 billion.

2

What We Know about Hurricanes

The violent storms called hurricanes, typhoons and cyclones are members of the same dreaded family; the only difference is in the names by which these greatest of earth's storms are known in the Western and Eastern Hemispheres.

Until quite recently the birth of the monstrous storms was explained very simply. It was said that they formed when there was a greater than usual upsurging of hot, moist air over tropical seas. When hot air rises, the moisture in it is condensed and towering clouds develop. It was assumed that the hurricane formation was completed when the clouds were whirled around the storm's center by the twisting forces of the earth's rotation.

This explanation left many unanswered questions. The one that puzzled scientists the most was the sharp drop in atmospheric pressure that is characteristic of all hurricanes.

Atmospheric pressure (the weight of air) is measured with a barometer. Just as water runs downhill, air moves from an area of higher pressure to one of lower pressure. The greater the difference in the atmospheric pressure in adjoining areas, or, as scientists say, the steeper the pressure gradient, the harder the wind blows. In the tropics, a barometer at sea level ordinarily registers about 30 inches of pressure; during one violent hurricane in Florida the barometer fell to 26.35 inches, the record low reading in the United States.

Most Atlantic Ocean, Gulf of Mexico and Caribbean Sea hurricanes develop between June and November. The hurricane season coincides with changes in the general circulation of the earth's atmosphere and the increase in the temperature of seawater. Until the water reaches a temperature of about 80° (warm even for tropical seas), hurricanes do not form. Research indicates that in years when the water is warmer than average there are more hurricanes. Such storms do not form along the east or west coasts of South America because the water adjacent to those coasts is relatively cold.

Summer in the Northern Hemisphere and the hurricane season begin when the earth is tipped toward the sun so that its direct rays strike farther north on earth. The obvious result is an increase in the temperature of the air. But there is also a change in the flow of air. The two great planetary wind systems, the northeast and the southeast trade winds, move north of their winter paths near the equator. The zone where these wind systems converge, known to sailors as the doldrums, also shifts northward. In the days of sailing ships the doldrums were dreaded, for in these regions of light and variable winds ships might drift for days.

Another atmospheric change during the summer is the return of a semipermanent zone of high pressure centered near the Bermudas, a group of islands about 1,000 miles east of Savannah, Georgia. "The Bermuda-Azore High," as the zone is usually called because it extends as far east as the Azore Islands off the

African coast, dominates the weather in the Northern Hemisphere in summer and fall. When the Bermuda-Azore High is strong it blocks the northerly movement of hurricanes.

The modern theory of hurricane formation developed from observations made in the late 1930s by Gordon E. Dunn, then chief of the U.S. Weather Bureau at Miami, Florida. Dr. Dunn noted that weather data reported by ships indicated a procession of atmospheric waves moving westward in the trade winds. The crests of such waves (high pressure areas) may be hundreds of miles apart and between the crests are troughs of low pressure. Further study by Dr. Dunn and other experts pointed to a relationship between the troughs and hurricanes.

During the hurricane season at least one low pressure trough passes each day over some part of the tropical Atlantic Ocean and Caribbean Sea, yet most of them do not develop into hurricanes. In addition to a trough of low pressure there must be a combination of other atmospheric conditions to trigger the formation of a hurricane.

Although the exact role played by each of these conditions is not yet understood, scientists have worked out a generalized picture of hurricane generation. The effect of high altitude winds is thought to be especially important.

At the ocean surface, hot moist air rushes into the low pressure trough, whooshes up and is cooled and condensed. Condensation of the moisture releases large amounts of heat energy that fuels the storm's "engine." If the heat energy released by a mature hurricane in one day were converted to electricity it would be enough for the electrical needs of the United States for more than six months.

If there are no strong high altitude winds to pump away the ascending air, the developing storm is choked by the hot air drawn into it at low levels. But if the ascending air is carried away by high altitude winds, the hurricane is nourished by the inflowing hot air and grows in size and intensity. Winds at 30,000 feet and at even higher altitudes provide the required exhaust mechanism for the air that has surged upward in the storm. Scientists know from the data on upper level winds, supplied by fliers and unmanned aerial instruments, when conditions aloft are favorable or unfavorable for a storm to intensify.

Warm air is lighter than cold air, which a barometer indicates by registering decreased pressure. Air of high heat content is carried to great elevations in the eye of a hurricane and it is these towering columns of hot air that account for the extremely low barometric readings at the surface. One of the measurements made to determine the intensity of a storm is the temperature of the air at different levels in the eye of the storm.

The structure of a hurricane is unique. No other storm has a calm core or eye around which air swirls upward like smoke through a chimney. The eye of an average hurricane is about 14 miles in diameter but eyes twice that size are not unusual. The wind and rainbands encircling the eye may cover an area more than 100 miles in diameter and their effect may extend for thousands of square miles. Unlike other storms, which have a short life span, hurricanes may live for weeks.

The fiercest wind howls around the eye of the hurricane. Here, as in the entire hurricane, the wind blows counterclockwise. (In the typhoons of the Southern Hemisphere the wind blows clockwise.) Since the wind is circling around, the direction from which it strikes any particular place on land or sea varies, as William C. Redfield, a self-taught American scientist, observed in 1821 when he traveled from Connecticut to Massachusetts soon after a hurricane.

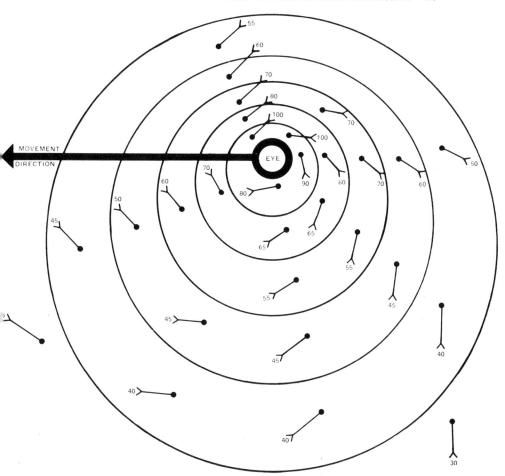

Wind circulation around a 100-knot hurricane. A knot is a unit of speed equivalent to 1 nautical mile (6,080 feet) per hour or about 1.15 land miles. Therefore, a 100-knot wind is blowing at 115 miles per hour. © 1965 by the United States Naval Institute, Annapolis, Maryland. Reprinted with permission.

At the beginning of his journey Redfield noted that the blown-down trees lay with their tops pointing northwest and that farther on the tops of the uprooted trees pointed southeast. The difference in the direction in which the trees pointed led

Redfield to conclude that hurricane winds do not blow from one direction but spiral around. The blown-down trees were Redfield's proof that hurricanes are rotary storms. After further study, Redfield wrote an article entitled "The Nature of Hurricanes" that was published in 1831 in the *American Journal of Science*. In the article Redfield explained that hurricanes consist of a large mass of air rotating rapidly around a calm center.

There is a dramatic lull during the passage of a hurricane's eye. The wind stops and the sun is visible through light clouds. It seems as though the storm is over. This calm has fooled many people. The official hurricane safety rules say, "Beware the eye of the hurricane. Stay in a safe place. Remember, at the other side of the eye, the winds rise very rapidly to hurricane force, and come from the opposite direction."

The wind is strongest in the front semicircle of a hurricane for there the wind's speed is increased by the movement of the storm itself. Thus, if at a point on the front semicircle the wind is blowing at 150 miles an hour to the north, and the hurricane is moving to the north at 60 miles an hour, the result is a 210 mile-per-hour wind.

Ships at sea maneuver to keep clear of the dangerous front semicircle where the wind is most violent and the waves highest. To succeed in this maneuver navigators must know the course on which the storm is traveling. This information is included in weather reports, and experienced navigators can also judge the position of their ship, relative to the storm's center from the direction of the wind and the waves.

Scientists cannot yet give a definite answer to how much of a hurricane's forward movement comes from the storm's own power system and how much from external forces. While developing, many hurricanes move slowly westward in the trade winds and then come under the control of other winds. It is now believed that high altitude winds play an important role not only in the growth of hurricanes but also in controlling the course on which hurricanes travel.

When a hurricane heads north, the rotation of the earth should cause the storm to curve to the right, which is to the east. The effect of the earth's rotation, known as the Coriolis force (the French scientist, Gaspard G. Coriolis, first described it) increases from the equator, where it is zero, to the poles. But the Coriolis force may be canceled out by atmospheric conditions. Predicting the course on which a hurricane will travel is exceedingly difficult.

Scientists who have mapped the courses of many hurricanes have found that no two have traveled exactly the same path. Hurricanes may make a complete loop and travel on a reverse course. It is not unusual for a hurricane to remain stalled in about the same position for days and then quite suddenly to accelerate. Hurricane Carol, of 1954, which killed about 600 in New England and caused tremendous property damage, was going lazily along at 5 miles an hour but as she approached the New Jersey coast speeded up to 70 miles an hour. Before people could prepare, the storm hit.

Weathermen know how hurricanes generally move during different periods of the hurricane season. But a general picture does not tell how any one storm will act.

While a storm is over a warm sea, the upward flow of hot moist air provides fuel for the hurricane's power system. When a hurricane passes over an island it is cut off briefly from its power source and the friction exerted by land also has a weakening effect, but ordinarily storms do not die while transiting an island.

Three of a series of satellite pictures showing the development of Hurricane Agnes in 1972.   NOAA

On June 17, Agnes was causing heavy rain in Cuba and her clouds extended to Florida.

By June 18, Agnes had intensified and had moved into the Gulf of Mexico. The eye of the storm was west of Florida.

AGNES

On June 19, Agnes made her landfall in Florida and clouds from the storm extended as far as Virginia.

However, hurricanes cannot survive when their course takes them over continents. Eventually the hurricane's engine stops for lack of fuel. But sometimes the remnant of a hurricane merges with a continental storm and adds to its power.

Even when dying, a hurricane may continue to be a killer as in the case of Camille. As a storm travels over land it may drop such torrential rains that large areas are flooded. The deaths and property damage resulting from flooding may be as great, or greater, than the losses caused along the coast by hurricane force winds and waves. Hurricane Diane of 1955 did little damage along the coast of North Carolina where it made its landfall, but subsequently rain from the storm caused flooding in Pennsylvania and New England that killed 200 and caused property damage estimated at $700 million.

Gauges cannot accurately measure the rainfall from a hurricane, for the wind blows the rain horizontally and only about half falls into the tube in the gauge. To get a realistic picture of hurricane rainfall one must about double the recorded figures. With this in mind, try to visualize the deluge on the West Indies island of Jamaica in 1909 when the rain gauges showed more than 8 feet of water. The rain continued for four days. Low-lying sections in a deluged area are always most severely affected, for in addition to the rain that falls directly on them flood water runs down from higher places.

3

Columbus Discovered Hurricanes

The term hurricane comes from a word Indians used for the savage storms that roar in from the sea. On the West Indies islands where Christopher Columbus first landed, the storms were called *huracan*, meaning evil spirit. Until white men came to America they had had no experience with such storms and they also called them *huracans*.

Hurricanes played important roles in Columbus's voyages of discovery. During his first voyage, it was probably a hurricane far to the south of his course that helped to make the voyage a success; during the second, a hurricane sank three of the explorer's ships; when a hurricane struck on his fourth and last voyage, Columbus, who by then had had experience with such storms, managed to save his fleet.

On the first voyage, the wind drove the *Niña*, the *Pinta*, and the *Santa María* westward, day after day. The direction of the wind was always about the same, which worried the sailors. The wind, blowing toward the west was fine for sailing west, but not for sailing east, and the ships would have to travel east to return to Spain. The sailors became panicky when the wind died and, while the ships drifted on a mirrorlike sea, Columbus's crew plotted a mutiny.

In his record Columbus wrote, "The people grumbled, saying that since there was no heavy sea that proved it would never blow hard enough to return to Spain." The grumbling stopped when the ships were rocked by great swells. Lookouts perched at the top of the masts could see no end to the surging waves. Columbus noted, "The sea made up considerably and without wind, which astonished them."

Present knowledge makes it seem likely that the swells came from a distant hurricane. The violent winds of such storms whip up swells that travel hundreds of miles from the storm's center. September 23, the date when swells rocked Columbus's fleet, is hurricane season in the area where the ships were located. If the storm had engulfed the fleet, Columbus might not have survived to discover America. The explorer was unaware of his good luck for he knew nothing about hurricanes. He learned about them on his later voyages.

When Columbus returned to Spain in the spring of 1493 he was hailed as a hero. The king and queen gave him the title Admiral of the Ocean Sea, and were so pleased with his account of "the Indies" that they directed him to begin preparations for a second voyage. Columbus asked for enough ships to transport colonists, soldiers and priests and was impatient with the delays in assembling a fleet of seventeen ships. He had planned to leave Spain in mid-August and to start by September 1 from the Canary Islands on the ocean crossing. On his first voyage he had started from the Canaries on September 6 and had had good weather. Columbus believed he would have equally good weather if he scheduled his second voyage for early September. We now know that September is not a good month for a voyage

Ships of this type carried soldiers and colonists across the Atlantic from Spain to the settlement at Santo Domingo.   The New York Public Library Picture Collection

from the Canary Islands to the West Indies because the possibility of encountering a hurricane is great. The delays that prevented Columbus from departing until October 13 were lucky, for by then the hurricane season was almost over.

When he arrived at the island he called Isla Española where he had left a fort and a small garrison, Columbus faced his first disaster in the New World. The Indians had burned the fort and killed all the Spaniards. The island, now known as Hispaniola, is occupied by the Dominican Republic and Haiti.

It was urgent that a settlement be established quickly so that the colonists could move from their cramped quarters on the ships. The scouts Columbus sent out to look for a site made several recommendations. One was at Cape Haitien on the northwest tip of the island where there is an excellent harbor. Columbus decided against Cape Haitien because it was too far from the gold mines the Indians had told him about. The site he chose on the south coast of Hispaniola was near the mines, according to the Indians, but it did not have a harbor. His ships simply anchored in front of the settlement. Several years later, the lack of a protected harbor cost Columbus three of his ships during a hurricane.

The colony was named Isabella in honor of the Spanish queen and, after devoting months to administrative work and expeditions into the surrounding country, Columbus appointed a council to govern Isabella, and left on a five-month voyage of exploration.

While Columbus was exploring, things went from bad to worse at Isabella. Little gold was found and the colonists, who had expected to get rich quickly, were in revolt. Some were on their way back to Spain before Columbus returned to Isabella. The unsuccessful fortune hunters blamed Columbus for everything that had gone wrong, and when they reached Spain told slanderous tales about the explorer. Instead of going back to present the true facts, Columbus stayed in Isabella trying to cope with the colonists and the Indians. By the spring of 1495, Columbus decided it was time to report directly to Ferdinand and Isabella, but before he could start a hurricane struck and three of his ships went to the bottom.

According to Peter Martyr, a courtier at the royal palace who wrote a history of the times, "There rose such a boisterous tempest of wind from the southeast as hath not lately been heard of. The violence hereof was such that it plucked up by the roots whatsoever great trees were within the force thereof. When the whirlwind came to the haven (harbor) of the city, it beat down to the bottom of the sea three ships which lay at anchor."

Only Columbus's flagship, the *Niña*, survived the storm. It was the first real hurricane that Columbus experienced.

Soon afterward Columbus sent out an exploring party to find a new site for a colony. One of his requirements was that it have a good harbor in which ships would have a chance to live through great storms. The exploring party was enthusiastic about a site on the south coast of Hispaniola which, they said, not only had a good harbor but gold-bearing rivers and rich soil for farming. Before Columbus sailed for Spain in March 1496, he ordered that a settlement be built on the site. Named Santo Domingo, it became the first permanent settlement of white men in America.

Except for the hurricane, Columbus would have arrived in Spain nearly a year before he did, and his enemies would have had that much less time to tell their lies. Despite them, Ferdinand and Isabella agreed to provide Columbus with a fleet of six vessels for a third voyage during which he discovered South America.

While Columbus was in America, the gossipmongers con-

The wreck of the Santa Maria *during Columbus's first voyage to America inspired an artist to paint this picture in 1892.*

tinued talking about the mismanagement at Santo Domingo, and Ferdinand and Isabella decided that the situation should be investigated. They appointed a royal commissioner and sent him to Santo Domingo. Shortly after he arrived he ordered that Columbus be arrested, manacled and sent back to Spain for trial.

The king and queen freed Columbus but they appointed another man governor of the Indies and kept Columbus waiting
two years before providing four ships for his fourth, and last,
voyage. He sailed with strict orders not to stop at Santo Domingo on his outward voyage, probably because Ferdinand and

Isabella thought there might be trouble between Columbus and the new governor.

However, when Columbus was nearing Santo Domingo, he recognized the signs of an approaching hurricane—large swells, high thin clouds racing across the sky, a crimson sunset, beautiful but menacing—and he hoped to take refuge in Santo Domingo harbor. He sent in a small boat with a note to the governor, in which he told of the oncoming storm. He asked permission to enter the harbor and urged that the fleet of thirty ships preparing to depart for Spain wait until the storm had passed. Not only did the governor refuse to permit Columbus to take shelter in the harbor but he scornfully rejected the advice to delay the departure of the homeward bound fleet.

The hurricane struck the fleet soon after it left Santo Domingo. Twenty ships, including the flagship, sank or were wrecked on the shore. More than 500 people were drowned. The flagship's cargo of gold, including the biggest nugget ever found in the West Indies, was lost. The only ship that weathered the storm and continued to Spain was a small one carrying gold that belonged to Columbus. There was enough of it to enable Columbus to live comfortably during the rest of his lifetime.

When he was refused permission to enter Santo Domingo harbor Columbus led his fleet of four ships to a place where the land provided some shelter but, during the hurricane three of the ships were torn from the anchorage. However, all survived the storm.

After giving his men a short period to rest, Columbus continued his voyage and explored the coast of Central America. Although his difficulties were by no means over, Columbus fortunately did not encounter another hurricane.

Map based on an old woodcut (1550) of *Hispaniola showing the location of Santo Domingo and Cape Haitien.* The New York Public Library Picture Collection

4

Some Hurricanes that Shaped American History

During the years when Santo Domingo was the only large Spanish settlement in the West Indies, it seemed to the people who lived there that their town was the target of all hurricanes. A bad storm in 1508 was followed by an even worse one in 1509 that destroyed almost every building in Santo Domingo.

The colony seemed to its inhabitants to be singled out for these disasters because they had no way of knowing about hurricanes that struck unpopulated places. Not until other settlements were established in the West Indies and on the North American coast did people learn that hurricanes rampage over a wide area.

Experience taught colonists and seafarers the signs that foretell the approach of a hurricane. The West Indies are in the path of the northeast trade winds and normally there is little variation in the wind's speed and direction. But before a hurricane the wind blows in gusts that become increasingly violent and they may come from any quarter. The clouds thicken and veil the sky. The waves that crash on the beach are bigger than the usual surf and the interval between the waves is longer.

The first official report of conditions during a West Indies hurricane was written by Cabeza de Vaca. The account of his experiences in the New World, prepared for the King of Spain, became a guide for later Spanish explorers who went to America.

In 1527 Cabeza de Vaca had sailed from Santo Domingo to Trinidad, Cuba to purchase horses for a gold hunting expedition on the North American mainland. As he was about to leave his ship to bargain for the horses, the captain pointed out to him the natural warning signs of an approaching hurricane and urged that he finish his business quickly. Cabeza de Vaca noted in his diary that the weather was "ominous." Before he went ashore, he left orders that if the wind increased, the ships should be run up on the beach and the men should get off. It was impossible to carry out these orders because when the storm hit, the wind drove the boats out to sea.

Cabeza de Vaca and the men who had gone ashore with him could find no shelter from the terrible storm. In describing his experience he wrote: "The rain and storm increased in violence at the village as well as on the sea and all the houses and the churches fell down and we had to go about, seven or eight men locking arms at a time, to prevent the wind from carrying us off, and under the trees it was no less dangerous than among the houses for as they also were blown down we were in danger of being killed beneath them."

There are many other references to hurricanes in the history of the colonization of America, and in a number of instances the course of events was changed by the intervention of a hurricane.

After the conquest of Mexico and Peru, the gold, silver and other treasures taken from the conquered lands made Spain the richest and most powerful nation in Europe. She claimed, by the right of discovery, vast territory in the New World and, to maintain her hold on it, sent out colonists to establish settlements.

In June 1559, 1,000 colonists and 500 soldiers sailed for the part of the North American mainland that Spain called Florida. The ships arrived in August on Florida's northwest coast and anchored near the site where afterward Pensacola was built. Before the colonists started to build homes, while they were still living aboard the ships, a hurricane struck. Many of the ships sank and hundreds of people drowned. Hurricanes were familiar terrors to Spaniards already living in America, but the one that struck in June 1559 convinced King Philip II of Spain that the west coast of Florida was too dangerous to settle and he directed that a site for a colony be found on Florida's east coast. Later the Spanish learned that Florida's east coast is also hurricane country.

Spain's losses from hurricanes were high but one storm helped Spain to retain possession of Florida. Except for that storm, France instead of Spain would have controlled the southeastern part of what is now the United States. In the spring of 1562 a daring French admiral, Jean Ribaut, landed in Florida near the St. Johns River (he called it the River of May) and claimed the land for France. Ribaut continued north along the coast and, near the present site of Port Royal, South Carolina, he built a small settlement named Charlesfort. Then Ribaut returned to France. When Spain learned about the settlement it organized an expedition to drive out the French. The Spaniards burned Charlesfort and killed the men who had been left to guard it.

France was not ready to give up. A fleet of French fighting ships sailed for America and Fort Caroline was built where Jacksonville, Florida now stands. The intention was to make

Fort Caroline a permanent settlement and Ribaut sailed there with soldiers and colonists. Since the water near the shore is shallow, the French anchored their ships offshore and used small boats as ferries to bring colonists and provisions to the fort. The ferrying was interrupted by the arrival of a Spanish fleet.

When the Spaniards saw that they were outnumbered they turned tail and sailed south for their settlement at St. Augustine. Ribaut followed quickly: his strategy was to attack before the Spanish were ready, but the battle did not take place. A hurricane destroyed Ribaut's ships. The men who managed to reach shore were rounded up by the Spanish and killed. Although for many years afterward the French raided Spanish settlements, the destruction of Ribaut's armada by the hurricane left Spain in possession of the southeastern part of North America.

Of the many hurricanes that have affected the course of history, none had as important an indirect result as the storm that struck the West Indies island, St. Croix, on August 31, 1772. Due to that hurricane Alexander Hamilton became a citizen of the United States. He was born on one of the smaller British West Indies islands and moved to nearby St. Croix when he was offered a job there. At the time of the storm he was only fifteen years old, but he was so skillful in handling business matters that his employer was glad to have him act as manager. If Hamilton had remained in St. Croix he might have become a wealthy merchant. The 1772 hurricane led to a different career for him.

Soon after the storm Hamilton sent a long letter about it to his father. He wrote:

I take up my pen just to give you an imperfect account of one of the most dreadful hurricanes that memory, or any records whatever, can trace, which happened here on the 31st ultimo at night.

It began about dusk, at north, and raged very violently till ten o'clock, then ensued a sudden and unexpected interval, which lasted about an hour. Meanwhile the wind was shifting round to the southwest point, from whence it returned with redoubled fury and continued so till near three o'clock in the morning. Good God! What horror and destruction—it is impossible for me to describe—or you to form any idea of it. It seemed as if a total dissolution of nature was taking place. The roaring of the sea and wind—fiery meteors flying about in the air—the prodigious glare of almost perpetual lightning—the crash of the falling houses—and the ear-piercing shrieks of the distressed were sufficient to strike astonishment into Angels.

He summed up the devastation caused by the storm by saying, "Misery in all its most hideous shapes spread over the whole face of the country."

Hamilton's father thought the letter so excellent that he proudly showed it to his friends and sent a copy of the letter to the editor of the St. Croix newspaper who printed it. The letter focused attention on Alexander Hamilton, and a group of men decided that the boy should have a chance to go to college. They raised enough money to pay for Hamilton's education at King's College (now Columbia College) in New York City.

During the American Revolution, Hamilton served as an aide to George Washington and after the war played a leading role in the adoption of the United States Constitution. As the first Secretary of the Treasury, Hamilton set the country on a sound financial basis. For Hamilton, and the United States, the 1772 hurricane was an ill wind that blew some good.

A storm that struck six years later, during the American

Revolution, prevented the Americans and their French ally from carrying out a plan to capture Newport, Rhode Island. Newport was being used by the British as a base for its naval operations on the New England coast.

The allies' plan provided for an attack from land and sea. The American army, reinforced by French marines, was to strike on the land side while the French fleet attacked from the sea. If the strategy had succeeded and the British had lost Newport, the war for independence might have been shortened.

However, just before the French marines were to have landed, the wind began to blow hard and the sea to build up. A hurricane was approaching. It had made its landfall in North Carolina and then had moved northward along the coast. Not only did the storm make the amphibious landing impossible but the commander of the French fleet hurriedly ordered his ships to sea. During a hurricane ships are in greater danger near shore than at sea where there is room to maneuver. The plan to take Newport had to be abandoned.

At sea the French sighted an English fleet. It was smaller than the French fleet and in normal weather could have been defeated by the French. But the men on the French ships were so busy cutting away broken masts and doing everything possible to save their ships that there was no battle and the English fleet escaped, suffering only, as did the French, from the storm.

The fear of hurricanes plagued both the French and English navies during the Revolutionary War and almost deprived the Americans of their victory at Yorktown. The British troops under General Cornwallis were concentrated at Yorktown, which is located on Chesapeake Bay. A French fleet under Admiral François de Grasse had been blockading the bay and Washington was anxious to attack from land while the French ships both bombarded Cornwallis's army and prevented its escape by sea.

According to Samuel Eliot Morison, the eminent historian, Admiral de Grasse was "apprehensive of hurricanes" and wished to depart before the attack on Yorktown. Washington visited the French admiral on his flagship, *Ville de Paris* and persuaded him to delay his departure.

On September 27, the day before the siege of Yorktown began, Washington sent a note to the admiral in which he wrote, "The resolution that your Excellency has taken in our circumstances proves that a great mind knows how to make personal sacrifices to secure important general good."

Thus Washington's plan of battle was successfully carried out. On October 17, 1781 Cornwallis ran up the white flag and two days later surrendered his army. The colonies had won independence.

During World War II, a typhoon in December 1944 crippled the task force of the United States Pacific Fleet that was to support the Army's invasion of the Philippines and the invasion was postponed. Some commentators believe that, except for the storm, the United States would not have used the atom bomb against Japan. If the invasion had been carried out as planned and the Philippines had been retaken, the war against Japan might have ended sooner and there would have been no need to drop the bomb.

During the storm, three destroyers capsized and sank with the loss of practically every man on board, nine other ships sustained serious damage and nineteen others less damage. One hundred forty-six planes were destroyed or damaged beyond repair—by fire, by being hurled around and smashed, and by being swept overboard. The loss of life totaled 790.

On October 19, 1781, General Cornwallis surrendered his army at Yorktown. George Washington's troops were aided by a French fleet under Admiral de Grasse.   The New York Public Library Picture Collection

A few months after the storm, Admiral Chester W. Nimitz, Commander-in-Chief of the Pacific Fleet, addressed a confidential letter entitled "Damages in Typhoon, Lessons of" to the officers of his fleet. After a brief summary of the havoc caused by the storm Admiral Nimitz stated: "The important thing is for it never to happen again."

The Navy's radioed weather news had not covered an area of some 300 miles in diameter where the storm was centered; but, said Admiral Nimitz, the lack of radioed storm warnings was no excuse for the ships to be unaware of their danger. He pointed out that "A hundred years ago, a ship's survival depended almost solely on the competence of her master and on his constant alertness to every hint of change in the weather. Seamen of the present day should be better at forecasting weather at sea, independent of the radio, than were their predecessors. The general laws of storms and the weather expectancy for all months of the year in all parts of the world are now more thoroughly understood."

The letter concluded with the direction that all officers of the Pacific Fleet should restudy the Navy's standard texts on storms and the handling of ships in heavy weather.

Until weather satellites were put into orbit there was no way of knowing about a hurricane that formed in a part of the ocean where there were no ships or planes. Today, pictures taken by satellites enable forecasters to locate and track hurricanes. Although it is unlikely that an American naval fleet will ever again be caught off guard by a hurricane, Admiral Nimitz's admonition to his officers is still valid. The commander of a ship is on his own during a storm and must know what to do.

5

A Tour of the National Hurricane Center

Anyone who wishes to visit the National Hurricane Center in Miami, Florida, can do so by making advance arrangements. During conducted tours, visitors see the Center's array of remarkable electronic equipment, which includes a receiver of relayed satellite pictures transmitted from 22,300 miles above the earth. The pictures are sent from space, line by line, in much the same way as an ordinary television transmission except that only one line at a time appears on the screen. In the satellite pictures a line represents a strip of the earth about 3 miles wide. When a picture is being received at the Hurricane Center, each line looks like a squiggle of tiny lighter and darker spots on the small round screen of the receiving set. A sensitized film inside the receiving unit is exposed to the varying shades of light in each line and after the more than 2,000 lines that comprise a picture have been received, the film is developed and prints are made. The pictures usually show the cloud formations over the entire Western Hemisphere. However, when the experts at the Hurricane Center suspect that a storm is forming, the "bird" can be commanded to focus its camera on a smaller area that the experts wish to watch closely.

The Center's large communications room resounds with the clatter of automatic teletypewriters that send and receive messages, many of them in code. Other instruments print out weather maps; 200 maps a day may be received from the National Meteorological Center near Washington, D.C., where giant computers digest the data needed for weather forecasting.

Many visitors find the Hurricane Center's radar room the most interesting part of their tour. Pointing to a group of pictures tacked on the wall, the radar expert, who is acting as guide, says, "These photographs are of famous ladies." They are photographs of hurricane formations as they were seen on the Center's radar screens. Each picture is labeled with the name of the storm and the date when it occurred. At first glance one picture looks much like the next, but upon closer inspection (and some hints from the radar expert) variations in the formations become apparent. For example, in one picture the eye is round and looks like a black hole in the center of thick whitish clouds and in another picture the eye is oval and the band of clouds surrounding it is wider in some areas than in others.

The Hurricane Center has one of the best land-based weather-search radars in the world. Its range is about 290 miles. However, since a radar beam travels in an almost straight line, and the earth is spherical, the farther outward the beam travels the higher it is above the earth. Toward the limits of its operational range, radar can only show targets thousands of feet aloft.

During a visit by a group of girls and boys to the Hurricane Center, a thunderstorm was in progress at Palm Beach 70 miles from Miami. The visitors could see the reflections of the droplets of rain on the radar screen. They appeared as greenish blobs.

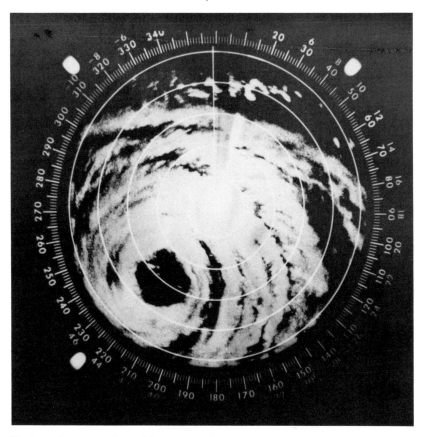

Radar photograph of Hurricane Betsy at 7:30 A.M. *on September 8, 1965 when the storm center was a little more than 60 miles from Miami. The distance between each of the concentric circles is 25 miles.* NOAA National Weather Service, NHC, Miami

*The radar dome on the roof of the National Hurricane Center build-
ing. The pole extending outward is the satellite receiving antenna.*
                                                                    NOAA

From them, experts can determine the intensity of the rain and
where it is falling. Data radar shows, plus information about
atmospheric conditions, enable weather experts to forecast the
areas the storm will affect.

The work of the National Hurricane Center is not limited to
the months of the hurricane season. Research continues all year
round. The actual paths that hurricanes traveled are compared

with the paths that were forecast. The detailed data collected by hurricane hunting planes and the National Weather Service's flying laboratories are analyzed to find why a storm acted as it did. Photographs of hurricanes taken by satellites are studied. The researcher can project the photographs in sequence (like a movie) or start with the last photograph and run the pictures backward to the first. Many hours may be devoted to a detailed examination of one photograph. The knowledge gained from studying hurricanes of the past is of tremendous value when weathermen are predicting the future course of an existing storm.

From June to November—the hurricane season—the specialists at the Hurricane Center keep a close watch on atmospheric disturbances from which a tropical storm may develop. The embryo of a hurricane may be detected first in a satellite picture of an area near the African coast. This is how Hurricane Irene of 1971 was spotted.

On September 7, satellite pictures showed cloud formations near Africa about which the experts were suspicious. Eight days later, the clouds were about 75 miles from South America and were moving northward, parallel to the coast. On September 17, a hurricane hunting plane reported that the disturbance had grown into a tropical storm. It was named Irene. Soon afterward Irene reached hurricane intensity. Irene was a unique hurricane. There is no record of any other Atlantic hurricane that acted as she did. Irene made her landfall on the east coast of Central America and crossed to the west coast. While overland Irene weakened but when she reached the Pacific she revived and grew into a Pacific Ocean hurricane. The storm died near Baja California, Mexico, on September 30. It caused heavy rain in southern California, Arizona and New Mexico.

A satellite picture taken on September 13, 1971 shows three active tropical storms, Edith in the western Gulf of Mexico, Fern over Mexico and Heidi, east of Cape Hatteras, North Carolina.   NOAA

News about a tropical disturbance far from land is included in forecasts of ocean weather and, depending on the reported conditions, ships and planes may detour to avoid the storm. Little or nothing is said about the storm in weather reports prepared for the general public. But if the disturbance continues to develop and to move toward land, the National Hurricane Center gives the storm a name and issues an announcement specifying the coastal areas to which the storm might be a threat. The naming of a storm transforms it from an impersonal force into a personality and focuses attention on it.

The custom of using girls' names for tropical storms originated during World War II. Other naming systems had previously been used. In Puerto Rico, hurricanes were named for the saints on whose feast days they occurred. Thus the storm that ripped through Puerto Rico on July 26, 1825 was known as the Santa Ana storm, and the one of September 13, 1876 as the San Felipe storm. In 1928, on the fifty-second anniversary of the San Felipe storm, Puerto Rico was again struck by a hurricane which was recorded as the second San Felipe. It killed 300 in Puerto Rico and 1,836 in Florida.

World War II weathermen originally used alphabetic labels for hurricanes. The first hurricane of a year was A, the second, B, and so on. Because of the difficulty of making a single letter understood in oral communications the phonetic alphabet was used: Abel for A, Baker for B, Charlie for C, Dog for D, etc. Then, for one reason or another, perhaps as a joke, tropical storms were given feminine names.

This custom was adopted officially in 1960 when the Weather Bureau prepared three lists of names, one for Atlantic, Caribbean and Gulf of Mexico storms, a second for tropical storms of the Eastern North Pacific and a third for those of the Central and Western North Pacific. Originally each list consisted of four separate sets of twenty-one names in alphabetic order except for Q, U, X, Y and Z, which were omitted because names starting with those letters are scarce.

In 1970, a new list of ten sets of names was adopted for Western Hemisphere hurricanes; during any ten-year period, no name will be used more than once. The Atlantic hurricane list, and the lists for Pacific Ocean storms contain 378 girls' names. In only a few instances is the same name included in the lists for Atlantic and Pacific storms. After all the sets comprising a list have been used, the list is recycled. (See pages 100–102 for the complete lists.)

When a name has been used for an especially great storm, such as Betsy of 1965 and Camille of 1969, the name is dropped from the list and a new name starting with the same letter is substituted.

One set of names is used each year, except in the Central and Western North Pacific where there are so many typhoons that a single set of 21 names may not be sufficient for the storms in any one year. Therefore, instead of starting a new set of names each year, all the names on the list are used consecutively. If the last typhoon in a year was Patsy, the first storm of the next year will be Ruth.

Of course, there is no reason why boys' instead of girls' names should not be used, as critics of the present system point out. But actually whether a storm is designated as a he, or a she, is of little consequence. No matter what it is named, a tropical storm is a monster.

Tension increases at the National Hurricane Center as a storm approaches land. The Center has the tremendous responsibility of forecasting the movement of storms in the Atlantic Ocean, the Gulf of Mexico and the Caribbean Sea. Atlantic hurricanes often make their first landfall on islands in the Caribbean and in these situations the first warnings issued by the Hurricane Center are for the islands in the storm's path. Information on which the predictions are based comes from many sources— weather stations on the islands, hurricane hunting planes, satellite pictures, ships, and the National Meteorological Center near Washington. Its computers, and the computers at the Miami weather office, are fed all the known facts about the storm and atmospheric conditions in a widespread area both at the surface and in the upper air. It does not take a computer long to print out its prediction.

Formerly forecasts were based on what experienced hurricane specialists believed would happen. Experts at the Center still prepare predictions and sometimes they differ from the computers. Then, before issuing a forecast, the hurricane specialists must decide whether they, or the computers, are right.

The accuracy of hurricane predictions has greatly improved in recent years. For the seventeen-year period from 1953 to 1970 the average error as to where a storm would be located twelve hours later was seventy-eight miles. In 1970 the average error was fifty-three miles.

A change in any one of the many atmospheric conditions that control the movement of a hurricane may cause it to act differently than the experts expected. In 1965, it was predicted that Hurricane Betsy, the first storm to cause damage amounting to more than a billion dollars, would make the sea rise 10 feet above normal in the Miami–Fort Lauderdale, Florida area. Many people evacuated homes near the waterfront. However, Betsy stayed farther offshore than the weathermen had expected and the storm tide was about 6 feet above normal. The sea flooded into some buildings, but not all that had been evacuated.

The cost of preparing for a hurricane is great and no one is more aware of this than the men responsible for forecasting. In a discussion of the problem, Dr. Robert Simpson, chief of the National Hurricane Center, said:

> The City of Miami requires a full twelve to eighteen hours to prepare adequately for a hurricane, and does so at a cost of more than three-quarter million dollars. A difference of only a few degrees in a storm's heading over a twenty-four hour period can mean that these expensive precautions will be made uselessly.

Betsy turned this street in New Orleans into a river. Only the roofs of the parked cars were above water.   American Red Cross photo by Rudolph Vetter

Yet the official policy, and a good one, is that errors should be on the side of overwarning and not underwarning.

The meaning of the terms used in the official reports must be understood to act upon them intelligently. For example, when a hurricane "watch" is issued for a specified area, it does not mean that preparations for storm conditions should be started immediately. A hurricane watch is a first alert that a storm poses a threat to an area during a stated period of time.

When the word, "watch" is changed to "warning" in the official advisories, it means that the hurricane is expected to strike within twenty-four hours. Most warnings give twelve to sixteen hours' advance notice but it may be less when, as sometimes happens, a storm suddenly speeds up.

In the areas for which hurricane warnings are in effect, most normal activities stop. Workers in factories and business offices are sent home. Schools are shut down. Homes near the waterfront are evacuated. If the storm threatens the Miami area, members of the Hurricane Center's staff are given time off to arrange for their families' safety and the protection of their homes. Then the staff goes on a "round-the-clock" work schedule. They may remain in the Center for days.

Preparations at the Center include bringing in a supply of food for its close to 100 staff members. All of the equipment in the Hurricane Center is checked, special attention being given to the emergency electric generator. It will provide the electric power the Center needs to function if the storm knocks out the municipal electric system. Some of the Center's doors are locked and signs saying Staff Only are tacked on other doors. The only outsiders admitted are reporters from radio and television stations and newspapers.

Official advisories and bulletins on hurricanes are concise

The "storm room" at the National Hurricane Center where data included in advisories and bulletins are analyzed.   NOAA

statements of what is known and what is expected. A headline summarizes the news. It is followed by short paragraphs stating the location of the storm, its size, intensity, the speed at which it is moving and its course. The areas that are threatened are named and advice is given as to the protective action to be taken both on land and sea. The tone of the report is calm. It ends with a restatement of the storm's position and the time when the next report will be issued.

The National Hurricane Center coordinates the flow of information to the public but not all of the advisories originate at the weather office in Miami. Depending on where the storm is located, official reports may be prepared in any one of four

An official report about a storm is broadcast from a weather station. Information about the movement of storms is updated at frequent intervals. NOAA

Hurricane Warning Offices located in Puerto Rico, New Orleans, Washington, D.C. and Boston. These offices are connected with the National Hurricane Center by a special hurricane teletype circuit through which they are supplied with data.

The Center depends for some of its information on volunteer observers who are members of CHURN (Cooperative Hurricane Reporting Network). Members are provided with an expensive set of instruments for measuring atmospheric pressure, the wind's speed, and rainfall. To be accepted as a member of CHURN, an applicant must live, or work, in an exposed position on the coast from which the weather service wishes reports and must undertake to perform his unpaid job until a storm destroys his instruments or endangers his life. There are more than 100 CHURN volunteers on the Gulf of Mexico and the east coast of the United States. The goal is to have CHURN stations spaced 25 miles apart.

An instruction sheet and forms for recording observations are provided to members of CHURN. During normal weather, observations are made once a day, usually at 7 A.M., and at the end of the month the record form is mailed to the local office of the National Weather Service. During hurricane emergencies observations are made at frequent intervals and are telephoned collect to the local weather station, which is linked by the teletypewriter circuit to the National Hurricane Center. If the local telephone service is disrupted by a storm, CHURN observers are instructed to send their reports by police radio or by any other available means.

When hurricane specialists are preparing predictions of the height to which a storm will raise the level of the water along the coast they always take into account the normal tides. Tables published by the National Ocean Survey list for every day of the year the times of high and low tides and, how many feet the water will rise and fall under ordinary conditions. Storm tides are most dangerous when they come at the time of normal high tide.

Atmospheric pressure affects the height to which the tide rises. When the pressure is high, it acts as a restraining force; the weight of the air presses down on the water. When the pressure is low the restraint is lessened and the water level rises. The sharp drop in the atmospheric pressure during a hurricane results in a sharp increase in the water level.

In addition, the breaking waves created by hurricane winds also increase the height to which the sea rises along the coast. The most rapid and greatest rise normally occurs on the part of the coast that is to the right of the path on which the storm is approaching land. Differences in the character of the sea bottom also affect how high the water rises. If the bottom slopes gently outward from the shore, hurricane tides are usually higher than in places where the slope is steep. It is a common mistake to think that a reef some distance from shore affords protection; actually, instead of serving as a breakwater, a reef tends to increase the flow of water inshore.

The National Hurricane Center supplements the information on the upper air collected by reconnaissance planes with frequent reports from automatic devices called radiosondes. A radiosonde is a small device (it weighs about 4 pounds) containing sensors for measuring air pressure, temperature and humidity, and a radio transmitter. As a radiosonde is carried aloft by a balloon, the measurements are transmitted to a receiving unit at the surface. By tracking the balloon, the speed and direction of the wind can be estimated. The balloon bursts at an altitude of approximately 20 miles, the radiosonde's parachute opens and the instrument drifts back to earth.

Most of the radiosondes launched from the Miami airport fall into the sea and sink, but a few years ago one made a parachute landing on Bimini, an island of the Bahama chain about 55 miles southeast of Miami. Another radiosonde released from an airport in the west landed in the backyard of the man who had sent it up.

Hurricane specialists continue to track tropical storms after they have moved inland and are no longer classified as hurricanes. As long as a storm is a threat to life or property, information about it is issued at regular intervals. Storms may live for weeks and, when they finally die, the hurricane specialists get ready for the work of tracking and forecasting the next one.

A radiosonde about to be sent aloft. The box contains sensors for measuring air pressure, temperature and humidity and a transmitter that radioes the measurements back to earth. NOAA

6

Flights into Hurricanes

For danger and thrills no flights can compare with those made by hurricane hunters. Other aircraft detour around storms; hurricane hunting planes fly into them.

"Being inside a hurricane can be like a bad dream," a pioneer of the hurricane hunting service said. He compared his experience in one storm with "going over Niagara Falls in a telephone booth."

Another pioneer hurricane hunter summed up his reactions by saying, "Don't ask me if I was scared or not. It would only be a fool or a liar who would say he wasn't worried."

Despite the hazards, only two hurricane hunting planes have been lost in the Atlantic area; one in 1942, the second in 1955 when a plane carrying a crew of eight and two Canadian newspapermen disappeared. The last contact with the plane was the pilot's report that he was flying into the hurricane at an altitude of 700 feet. After the storm abated, a wide area was searched but neither wreckage nor bodies were sighted. Every hurricane hunter knows that his chance of survival is practically nil if his plane falls into the storm-crazed sea.

There have been many near accidents. Planes have returned with rivets sheared from their wings and with heavy plexiglass windows bent in. Twelve feet were torn from one wing of a plane entering the eye of a hurricane. The aircraft was so torque-twisted that it was beyond repair, but it brought its crew back to their home base.

The first flight into a hurricane was made on July 27, 1943, in a small single-engine plane piloted by Colonel Joseph B. Duckworth. During World War II he was head of the Army's Instrument Flying Instructors' School at Bryan, Texas.

The history-making flight was a spur-of-the-moment affair. While Joe Duckworth was having breakfast at the field someone mentioned that a hurricane had been reported moving toward Galveston. Duckworth gave the news a few minutes' thought and then said to Lieutenant Ralph O'Hair, who was sitting opposite him at the table, "Let's go down and get an AT-6 and penetrate the center, just for fun." Official approval for the flight was not requested and probably would not have been given because of the risk involved.

O'Hair, a navigator, immediately said he would like to go and the men took off in the early afternoon. At first their only trouble was the static that made radio communication impossible. The static cleared up as the plane approached Houston and the fliers radioed to the airfield that they were heading for Galveston.

"Do you know that Galveston is being battered by a hurricane?" they were asked. The fliers said they knew and were going into it. "Please report back every little while," the radioman at the field requested.

Turbulence increased as the plane entered the clouds surrounding the storm's center. Within it the sky was clear and the ground below was visible. Duckworth nosed down to see where he was, but the air was so rough that he climbed again, flew around in the storm's center for a short time and then headed back for his base.

When the plane landed, the weather officer at the airfield, Lieutenant William Jones-Burdick, congratulated the men and said he was sorry that he had not been on the flight.

"OK," said Joe Duckworth, "hop in and we'll go back through and have another look." The weather officer's log of the flight gives a picture of what it was like.

As the plane entered the storm, the weather officer reported heavy rain and five minutes later that the clouds were becoming darker and more dense. In another entry, severe turbulence was noted. While the plane circled in the eye of the hurricane the air temperature was 73° but when the plane headed out of the storm the temperature fell to 46°. The scientific data collected was interesting, but the real importance of Duckworth's flights was that they proved that planes can penetrate hurricanes. Duckworth's flights revolutionized the tracking of tropical storms.

Before aircraft began to hunt hurricanes, weather forecasters had to depend on reports from ships and weather stations on land. Such reports can give conditions only in specific locations but planes can range over a large area. Atlantic hurricanes are stalked over 1.5 million square miles of ocean and gulf waters. From these flights such vital information as the size of the storm, the speed at which it is moving, the direction of its course, and the storm's maximum winds are obtained. Since scientists have been flying into hurricanes, the features of these monsters are no longer unknown mysteries. And when you know the nature of an enemy, strategies can be developed for fighting it.

Following Colonel Duckworth's two flights a few others were made during the 1943 hurricane season and at the end of it the Weather Bureau recommended to the Joint Chiefs of Staff that military planes be used regularly to track hurricanes. A plan for hunting hurricanes was approved in February 1944 by representatives of the Army Air Force, the Navy and the Weather Bureau. At the end of that year there was another meeting at which fliers, forecasters and the men who directed the hurricane hunting flights discussed how, in view of the year's experience, the service could be improved.

Since then many improvements have been made in weather planes and their scientific equipment. Hurricane fliers now do their hunting in huge four-engine planes with a fuel capacity for flights of about twenty-two hours (almost four times as long as it takes airliners to cross from New York to London). Normally a hurricane hunting plane spends six to ten hours in the storm area plus the flight time to the storm and back to the air base. Guided by the plane's radar, the pilot steers for the eye of the storm. After determining its location and size, measurements are made of the atmospheric pressure, the temperature of the air and its moisture content. The plane then collects data in other parts of the storm and before leaving it makes a second penetration of the eye. The speed at which a storm is moving is calculated from the change in the position of its eye. Ordinarily, air surveillance begins when a storm is about 300 miles from land.

The hurricane hunters of the Air Force and the Navy get their orders from CARCAH (Chief of Aerial Reconnaissance Coordination for Atlantic Hurricanes). Headquarters of the coordination unit is near the National Hurricane Center in

Navy hurricane hunting planes make low-level penetrations into storms. Only from the cockpit is there a full view of sea and sky.

Miami. The Center's weather experts decide on the flights they wish made on the following day either to probe a storm or to reconnoiter an area about which they are suspicious. Around noon a suggested schedule is given to CARCAH, which prepares and issues the flight plans.

Whether a flight is assigned to the hurricane hunters of the Air Force or the Navy depends on many considerations, but primarily on where the storm, or the area under suspicion, is located. Since the Army's weather planes are based at Ramey Air Force Base, Puerto Rico, and the Navy's at Jacksonville, Florida, flights over the open Atlantic east of Puerto Rico are normally assigned to the Army Air Force and flights in the Gulf of Mexico to the Navy.

The commanding officer of the squadron that is to make the flight decides which crew and plane is to fly the mission. Ordinarily crews get time off between assignments but sometimes the rest periods are brief. The Air Force plane that went into the eye of Hurricane Camille the morning after the great storm formed landed at Orlando, Florida, refueled and immediately took off for a second flight into Camille. Air Force medals were awarded to the commander and crew of the plane for these flights.

"The eye of an intense hurricane is often a spectacular cloud colosseum 20 to 40 miles in diameter," a hurricane hunter wrote recently. "Tier upon tier of cloud layers, arranged like seats in a gigantic amphitheater, extend upward more than 8 miles from the surface of the sea. Winds are light and variable and sometimes a ray of sunlight pokes a silvery finger down to the sea below."

Frequently pilots must battle to get through the black wall of clouds surrounding the storm's calm center. The technique is not to fly a straight course into the clouds but to enter them at an angle. In intense storms more than one attempt may be required to bore through the clouds. Three attempts had to be made by an Air Force plane to get into the center of Typhoon Gloria. At the time, the storm was about 50 miles north of Wake Island, an important aviation base in the Pacific. The flight into Typhoon Gloria was so perilous that the weather officer, Captain Al Gideons, an experienced "Typhoon Chaser," wrote a description of it under the title, "My Great Typhoon Story."

"The wall cloud" he wrote, "is a solid, circular band of heavy cumuloform clouds complete with thunderstorms, very strong winds, excessively heavy rain—we know we're in for a real jolt when we hit the wall cloud—it's massive. We tried to bore into the wall cloud. The airplane was literally tossed out and forced parallel to the wind flow around the wall cloud. OK, regroup. Try it again, this time crabbing (angling) into the wind more. Wham! Once again we're rejected by the wall cloud. Again we tried, this time with about a 40 degree crab into the wind. We slammed into the wall—yes, it sure seemed like a wall. The noise from the rain was deafening. Outside it looked like we were in a waterfall. Severe turbulence, the worst I've experienced. Nothing to do but hold on and hope the airplane stays upright. A minute or so later and we're through it. In the eye, total serenity, calm, smooth air, sunny, hot. And all around us that boiling storm."

Captain Gideons stated that at one point he thought it might be smart not to fly into the storm's eye but to determine its location by radar. Radar is frequently used for this purpose. However, radar cannot give the detailed information that is obtained by going into a storm and therefore, Captain Gideons's plane like most others that hunt hurricanes and typhoons, fought its way into the storm.

A weather plane is a flying laboratory, crammed with instruments capable of collecting and recording a vast variety of data from the maximum height of a storm's clouds to the temperature of the sea at, and below, the surface. Cloud heights are measured by a radar transmitting unit. The unit is mounted on top of the plane; its housing looks, according to one airman, "like storage

Hurricane Betsy taken from an Air Force plane flying more than 11 miles above earth. The circular structure of the clouds is typical of hurricane formations. USAF Air Weather Service

space for a giraffe." A more powerful unit, attached under the plane's fuselage, can "see" the clouds and rain in an area of about 200,000 square miles.

The temperature of the sea is taken by a remarkable device called a sonobuoy. It is launched from the plane and radioes back the temperature of the water at two second intervals. Each report tells the water's temperature 10 feet below the depth at which the previous measurement was made. No attempt is made to recover a sonobuoy; it is left in the sea.

Instruments on the plane automatically record atmospheric pressure, air temperature, wind speed and direction at the level

Radar men making a final check of their equipment before take-off time. Hurricane hunters rely on radar to locate the eye of the storm.
U.S. Navy Photograph

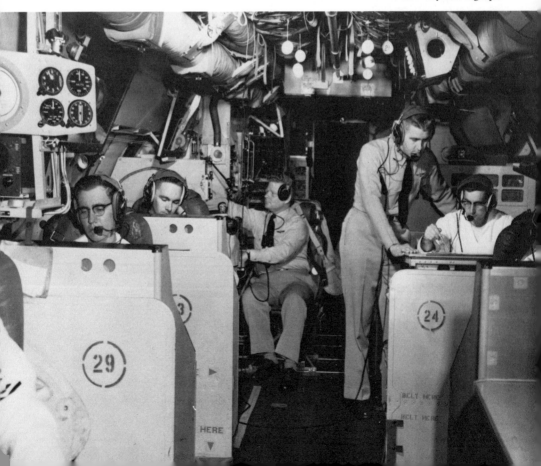

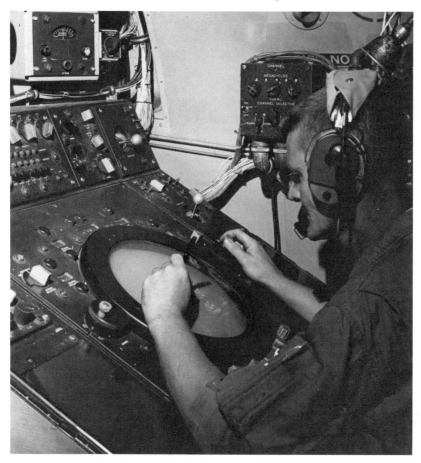

While the plane is flying toward a storm, the position of the storm's eye is plotted on a radarscope by one of the radar experts.   U.S. Navy Photograph

at which the plane is flying. To obtain the same information from lower levels, dropsondes are used. These parachute-borne canisters are released periodically through a pressure hatch in the plane. As a dropsonde descends, its sensors make measurements and its small radio transmits them in code to the plane. These and other measurements are fed to the plane's computer

The flight engineer's station showing the many dials and switches that he must continually monitor.

and the computerized data are sent by radio teletype to weather stations on land. Before a hurricane hunting plane lands, forecasters know how a storm is acting.

Hurricane hunting by the Air Force and the Navy differs in one respect. Navy planes make low level penetrations at 500 to 1,000 feet, which some aeronautical experts think is risky. However, the Navy's accident record has been good and from low level flights the state of the sea can be observed, information that the Navy needs for the protection of its surface ships. Air

Force planes fly into storms at 10,000 feet and climb to 30,000 feet or more for probes of the upper air. Flight plans specify the details of the hurricane hunting mission but pilots have discretion to vary a plan if conditions make it necessary to do so.

Hurricane hunting is the most dramatic duty of the Army and Navy weather planes. Therefore, comparatively little is written about the routine, but really important, daily flights made to collect information about weather developments over the ocean. The planes fly standard routes, called tracks, and the flight plan designates the points at which observations are to be made. The data collected includes: icing conditions aloft, the state of the sea at its surface, air pressure and cloud formations. This information is vital for weather forecasting.

During a hurricane hunting flight a photographic record is made of the formations shown by radar.   U.S. Navy Photograph

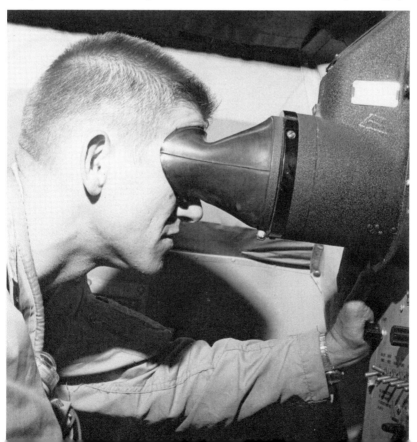

Routine weather flights are also made over the Pacific by planes based on the United States' West coast and on military airfields on Pacific Ocean islands. But in the areas where typhoons rage, the fliers know that any day of the year their assignment may be to explore a storm. The hurricane season is limited, but typhoons strike throughout the year.

7

Can Earth's Greatest Storms Be Tamed?

The scientists working on Project Stormfury have been trying to change the behavior of hurricanes. Their goal is to tame the monstrous storms by altering their structure so that they will weaken or destroy themselves.

The experimental work is based on years of intensive study of the mechanism and characteristics of tropical storms. Project Stormfury makes use of all of the available data on hurricanes; it sends its experts on flights into hurricanes to make firsthand observations and it conducts elaborate laboratory experiments.

Meteorologists have known for a long time that atmospheric pressure is lowest in the eye of a hurricane and that there is a sharp increase in pressure in the wall clouds ringing the eye. Because of this sharp difference in pressure, the air flowing toward the eye attains maximum speed in the wall clouds. If the pressure in the wall clouds could be lowered so that it would be about the same as in the eye, the natural result would be a decrease in the winds' speed and a dispersal of the energy concentrated about the center.

A weather plane is jammed with equipment and there is little space for the crew to move about. NOAA

How can atmospheric pressure be altered? Stormfury scientists believe that it can be done by increasing the heat in selected portions of a hurricane. In the experiments that have been conducted, chemicals have been scattered into clouds to freeze the water droplets in them. The freezing results in the release of heat energy into the storm system.

The first attempt to modify a hurricane by seeding it with chemicals was made in 1947 after successful experiments with seeding clouds similar to hurricane clouds. The 1947 experiment was privately financed and only one plane was used. Clouds in the hurricane were seeded with about 200 pounds of dry ice and since the effect was not monitored, nobody knew whether, or how much, freezing occurred.

However, some people blamed the seeding for the hurricane's change of course. Before the experiment, the storm had passed over southern Florida and then had headed back to sea. It was moving on a northerly course along the coast when the dry ice was dropped into it. Soon afterward the hurricane turned west and struck Georgia. There was talk of suing the scientists for the damage caused by the storm, but no lawsuits were actually brought. Government experts who made a complete study of the storm stated that its turn to the west could be attributed to natural conditions prevailing at the time of seeding. But the verdict might have been different if a judge and jury had been asked to decide whether the seeding had caused the hurricane to act as it did.

In order to avoid legal complications, a rule was adopted, when Stormfury was established in 1962, limiting the areas where experiments could be made. Modification experiments

The white areas on this drawing show where experiments on seeding hurricanes were originally authorized. NOAA

were authorized only in three areas: one in the southwest Atlantic, the second in the Caribbean Sea and the third in the Gulf of Mexico. Hurricanes that might reach a populated area within thirty-six hours were not to be seeded.

In 1963, Hurricane Beulah was seeded and changes were noted in the storm's structure. Until 1969 there was no hurricane eligible for a modification experiment. The restrictions have now been revised and experiments are permitted on storms not predicted to move closer than 50 miles to a land area within eighteen hours after seeding. When recommending the change in the restrictions, the advisory panel, composed of five meteorologists, concluded that the new rule would not increase the threat to life and property posed by hurricanes.

The 1969 experiment on Debbie was conducted under the old

Flight track of a plane during the seeding of a hurricane. The plane flies through the eye of the storm to reach the area specified for seeding.　　　　　　　National Hurricane Research Laboratory

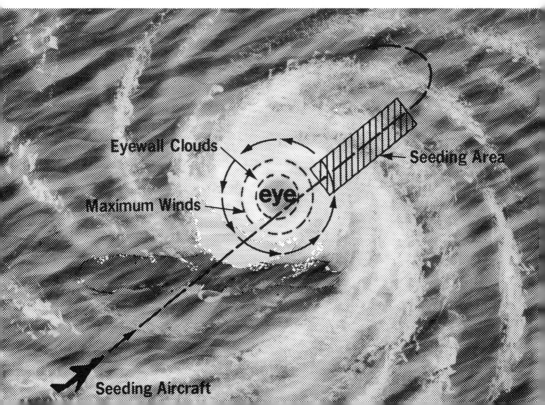

Painting showing (1) a seeding plane and (2) a plane monitoring the effects of the release of silver iodide into the clouds. NOAA

rules. The storm formed soon after Great Hurricane Camille and met the scientific requirements for a seeding experiment. Debbie was a mature hurricane with maximum winds of more than 115 miles an hour. However, she was located about 650 miles from the Puerto Rico airfield where the heavily instrumented weather planes were based. This distance was just within range for a seeding experiment. There is a limit to how far out planes can go because their fuel supply must be conserved for

Canisters containing silver iodide, fastened to an aircraft's wings, are released by a control within the plane. During the experiment on Debbie, thousands of canisters were dropped. Naval Photographic Center

the many hours that they will operate in the storm area.

Thirteen aircraft, nine Navy hurricane hunters, two from the Air Force, and two research planes from the National Weather Service, carried out the experiment on Debbie. Five of the planes did the seeding and the eight others served as monitors. The monitoring began four hours before the first seeding and continued until six hours after the last seeding. The monitoring planes flew at altitudes of 1,000 to 37,000 feet. The operational plan provided that each plane was to perform its assigned duty for a stated number of hours and then be relieved by another plane.

The seeding material was silver iodide, a chemical that causes freezing more effectively than dry ice and also is more convenient to use. With silver iodide, seeding can be done on a massive scale. During the Debbie experiment, the seeding planes dropped thousands of canisters filled with an inflammable solution containing particles of silver iodide. As the canisters fell and ignited, the silver iodide in the plumes of smoke was spread by the hurricane's winds.

The seeding was started after the plane had penetrated the wall clouds and was in the area of maximum winds. The seeding was continued as the planes flew out of the wall clouds into the adjacent rainbands.

Debbie was seeded on August 18 and on August 20. On both days five seedings were made at two-hour intervals on paths about 16 to 23 miles in length. The actual seeding took only two to three minutes and the planes flew at an altitude of 33,000 feet. The weather service's research planes made repeated passes across the storm at 12,000 feet. At this altitude, data collected in storms similar to Debbie, indicated that the winds would be about 95 percent as strong as at the surface. Before the first seeding on August 18, Debbie's winds at 12,000 feet were 112 miles an hour. The winds decreased in speed after the second and third seedings. Five hours after the fifth, and last, seeding the winds had decreased to 78 miles an hour or by a fraction over 30 percent.

On August 19, when there was no seeding, Debbie reintensified. The first planes that scouted the storm on August 20 reported that Debbie had developed two eyes, an unusual structure in hurricanes. There have not been enough experiments to determine whether the two eyes resulted from the seeding.

The winds did not diminish as much after the second day of seeding as after the first. The monitoring planes recorded winds of 113 miles an hour before the seeding was started and winds of 96 miles an hour after the final seeding. The official report of the experiment contains the cautious statement that: "It is not yet certain whether the decreases in wind speeds on the two

A hole more than 3 miles wide was created in a cloud bank by seed-ing it with only 11 pounds of silver iodide. National Hurricane Research Laboratory

days were caused by the seeding or whether they resulted from natural changes in the hurricane." Then the report says more positively: "That the storm's winds diminished on both seeding days strongly suggests that at least some of the changes were caused by the modification experiment."

Despite the cautious tone of the report, Stormfury scientists considered the experiment a real success. Not only had there been a decrease in the winds' speed but the Debbie experiment provided data for subsequent attempts to modify hurricanes. When the 1969 hurricane season ended, the scientists began to make plans for 1970. But in 1970 there were no storms suitable for experimental purposes.

In addition to the technique used on Debbie, Project Storm-fury scientists had developed two others for seeding clouds some distance from a storm's center: one, called Rainband, was de-signed for seeding a single band of clouds; the other, Rainsector, for seeding a number of bands.

Satellite photographs of Debbie on August 18, 1969, three hours after the seeding of the hurricane was started. NOAA

On August 19, when no seeding was done, the satellite's camera showed that the storm had reintensified. NOAA

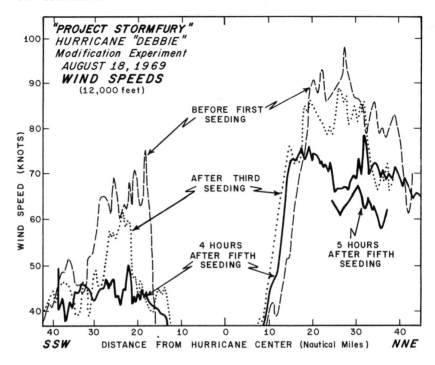

When Hurricane Ginger formed in the southeast Atlantic early in September 1971, and reconnaissance planes reported that the storm had poorly formed wall clouds, Stormfury scientists decided that the seeding technique used on Debbie was not appropriate. Instead, they experimented with their Rain-sector method. All of the bands of rain in one sector of the storm up to 100 miles from the eye were seeded.

The objective was to make the clouds increase in height until they reached the altitude at which air from the storm center was being carried away by high level winds. Ordinarily the warm moist air from rain clouds flows into the storm and strengthens it. If the natural pattern could be changed so that the warm moist air would balloon up and be wafted away, a major source of the hurricane's energy supply would be eliminated.

Everyone was disappointed that some of the seedings scheduled for the first day, September 26, had to be canceled because the plane directing the experiment had radar trouble. After a plane with working radar arrived, two seedings were completed. The seeding was done only when rain was hitting the windshield of the plane and it was climbing at least 500 feet a minute.

There was radar trouble again on September 28, the second day of the experiments, but the scheduled five seedings were made. Each lasted about 50 minutes. After these seedings Ginger's winds decreased from 90 to 79 miles per hour. Although Stormfury scientists said that natural forces might have caused the decrease, satellite pictures and radar showed definite changes in the structure of the clouds.

Ginger was an unusual hurricane. Her life span exceeded that of any other recorded hurricane. Ginger formed on September 5 and died on October 5. During this thirty-one day period Ginger was a full hurricane for twenty days. She moved slowly and sometimes seemed uncertain where to go. Before the seeding experiment, Ginger had looped back to the east and had also made a smaller loop to the south. Finally Ginger headed for the United States coast and on September 30 made her landfall in Morehead City, North Carolina. On the morning of October 3, Ginger went back to sea. By that time Ginger had weakened and was no longer a hurricane. Her classification had been downgraded to that of a tropical depression. She killed no one on land and the rain that fell from Ginger's clouds was beneficial. The coastal area in Ginger's path had been suffering from a water shortage.

Although there have been only a few opportunities to experi-

ment on hurricanes, Project Stormfury scientists have been test-
ing their techniques on the towering cumulous clouds that are
present almost every day of the year in the tropics. These clouds
have many of the same characteristics as hurricane rainband
clouds.

Project Stormfury scientists do not expect quick results, but
they are hopeful that from experiments in the sky and in laboratories a way will be found to curb the wild fury of hurricanes.

8

Anyone Can Track the Course of a Hurricane

The National Hurricane Center tracks the courses of all Atlantic hurricanes but if you live in hurricane country and a
tropical storm is heading your way, you can do your own tracking and judge if, and when, the hurricane may affect you.

Anyone can map the course of a hurricane by using a Tracking Chart and the information given in broadcast hurricane advisories and bulletins. Local offices of the National Weather
Service sometimes have copies of Tracking Charts and will supply one, or a chart can be ordered from the Government Print-
ing Office, Washington, D.C. 20402. A Tracking Chart costs 15
cents.

The chart covers the area from the Cape Verde Islands, near
Africa, to the Atlantic and Gulf coasts of the United States and
includes the islands of the Caribbean Sea, Mexico, Central
America and the northern coast of South America. The tropical
Atlantic, in the vicinity of the Cape Verde Islands, is a breeding
ground for hurricanes.

The Tracking Chart is drawn on a framework of latitude and

longitude lines 5 degrees apart. The horizontal latitude lines and the vertical longitude lines form squares that are divided into twenty-five smaller squares. The space between the bottom and top lines of the small squares represents 1 degree of latitude and the space between the side lines, 1 degree of longitude. However, since the official advisories and bulletins give the location of a hurricane's center to the nearest one-tenth of a degree you must approximate its position within the proper small square.

For example, assume that in the first advisory issued by the National Hurricane Center, the position of the storm's center is reported to be 13.9° north latitude and 56.1° west longitude. By counting three lines up from the horizontal line labeled 10° you are at 13° north latitude, and one line to the left of the vertical longitude line labeled 55° is 56° west longitude. Then you judge where to put your mark to show the additional fractions of latitude and longitude to map the storm's center as accurately as possible. Place the dot, circle, or cross that you have decided to use as a marker just below the 14° latitude line and just a little to the left of the 56° longitude line.

The mapping procedure is the same each time a new location of the storm's center is reported. After marking the new position on the Tracking Chart draw a line between the new position and the previous one. These track lines show the course on which the hurricane traveled. Track lines may be nearly straight or may include one or more loops when a storm meanders.

To give mapping more meaning, write the date and hour next to each position you enter on the Tracking Chart. Especially if the same chart is used for mapping more than one hurricane, each track line should be identified with the name of the storm. Using a different color for mapping each storm makes its track distinctive.

Hurricane bulletins and advisories state the direction in which a storm is traveling and its speed. As its future course is of the greatest importance, it is advisable to draw a dotted line on the chart showing where the hurricane will go if it travels its predicted course. Thus you are able to judge whether you are in a dangerous area or whether it is likely that the hurricane will pass you by.

In addition to notations on the track lines it is recommended that detailed data be listed in tabular form. For this purpose the official Tracking Chart includes a table with columns for the date and time of each reported position of the hurricane's center, maximum winds, the speed at which the storm is moving and in what direction. The last four columns are headed Forecast. In these columns you write, in abbreviated form, the predicted forward speed of the storm, the direction of its course, and whether the hurricane is expected to intensify or diminish. Pay close attention to the forecasts. If a hurricane is a threat to you it is vitally important to know how the storm is expected to act.

After a hurricane has died, it is interesting to compare its predicted course, indicated on your chart, with the storm's actual course. Hurricane experts spend a long time making such checks. The experts not only make a complete analysis of the storm but of the general atmospheric conditions during its life. These studies provide scientists with clues for increasing the accuracy of hurricane forecasting and with facts that some day may lead to a method for controlling the monster storms. Until then we must depend on advance warnings to protect ourselves from the killers. If a hurricane threatens the area in which you live, heed the experts' forecasts and be sure you know the safety rules for living through a hurricane.

APPENDIX I

Official Safety Rules

1. Enter each hurricane season prepared.

   Every June through November, recheck your supply of boards, tools, batteries, nonperishable foods, and the other equipment you will need when a hurricane strikes your town.

2. When you hear the first tropical cyclone advisory:

   Listen for future messages; this will prepare you for a hurricane emergency well in advance of the issuance of watches and warnings.

3. When your area is covered by a hurricane watch:

   Continue normal activities, but stay tuned to radio or television for all National Weather Service advisories. Remember: a hurricane watch means possible danger within twenty-four hours; if the danger materializes, a hurricane warning will be issued. Meanwhile, keep alert. Ignore rumors.

4. When your area receives a hurricane warning:

Keep calm until the emergency has ended.

Plan your time before the storm arrives and avoid the last-minute hurry that might leave you marooned or unprepared.

Leave low-lying areas that may be swept by high tides or storm waves.

Leave mobile homes. They are extremely susceptible to high winds and storm tides.

Moor your boat securely before the storm arrives, or evacuate it to a designated safe area. When your boat is moored, leave it, and don't return once the wind and waves are up.

Board up windows or protect them with storm shutters or tape. Danger to small windows is mainly from wind-driven debris. Larger windows may be broken by wind pressure.

Secure outdoor objects that might be blown away or uprooted. Garbage cans, garden tools, toys, signs, porch furniture, and a number of other harmless items become missiles of destruction in hurricane winds. Anchor them or store them inside before the storm strikes.

Store drinking water in clean bathtubs, jugs, bottles, cooking utensils; your town's water supply may be contaminated by flooding or damaged by hurricane floods.

Check your battery-powered equipment. Your radio may be your only link with the world outside the hurricane. Emergency cooking facilities, lights, and flashlights will be essential if utilities are interrupted.

Be sure your car is fueled. Service stations may be inoperable for several days after the storm strikes, due to flooding or interrupted electrical power.

Stay at home, if it is sturdy and on high ground. If it is not, move to a designated shelter, and stay there until the storm is over.

Remain indoors during the hurricane. Travel is extremely dangerous when winds and tides are whipping through your area.

Monitor the storm's position through National Weather Service advisories.

Beware the eye of the hurricane. If the calm storm center passes directly overhead, there will be a lull in the wind lasting from a few minutes to half an hour or more. Stay in a safe place unless emergency repairs are absolutely necessary. But remember, at the other side of the eye, the winds rise very rapidly to hurricane force, and come from the opposite direction.

5. When the hurricane has passed:

Avoid loose or dangling wires and report them immediately to your power company or the nearest law enforcement officer.

Seek necessary medical care at Red Cross disaster stations or hospitals.

Stay out of disaster areas. Unless you are qualified to help, your presence may hamper first-aid and rescue work.

Drive carefully along debris-filled streets. Roads may be undermined and may collapse under the weight of a car. Landslides are also a hazard.

Report broken sewers or water mains to the water department.

Take special care to prevent fires. Lowered water pressure may make fire fighting difficult.

Check refrigerated food for spoilage if power has been off during the storm.

Remember that hurricanes moving inland can cause severe flooding. Stay away from riverbanks and streams.

Tornadoes that are spawned by hurricanes are among the storms' worst killers. When a hurricane approaches, listen for tornado watches and warnings. A tornado watch means tornadoes are expected to develop. A tornado warning means a tornado has actually been sighted. When your area receives a tornado warning, seek inside shelter immediately, preferably below ground level. If a tornado catches you outside, move away from its path at a right angle. If there is no time to escape, lie flat in the nearest depression, such as a ditch or ravine.

Terms to Know

A TROPICAL CYCLONE is the internationally accepted term for any weather pattern of tropical origin in which the wind tends to blow, in a counterclockwise direction in the Northern Hemisphere, around a more or less well-defined low pressure center. In the Southern Hemisphere, the direction of the wind is clockwise.

TROPICAL CYCLONES are classified according to form and intensity as (1) TROPICAL DISTURBANCE, (2) TROPICAL DEPRESSION, (3) TROPICAL STORM and (4) HURRICANE or TYPHOON.

An ISOBAR is a line on a weather map connecting points of equal atmospheric pressure. Each point that an isobar crosses has the same pressure. Most isobars extend over large portions of a weather map and their two ends do not connect.

A CLOSED ISOBAR is shown as a circular line and connects points of equal pressure ringing the low pressure center of a storm.

A TROPICAL DISTURBANCE has no closed isobars. Winds at the surface are not strong, but aloft the rotary circulation may be better developed. Such disturbances are common in the tropics.

A TROPICAL DEPRESSION has one or more closed isobars and some rotary winds at the surface that may attain a speed of 39 miles an hour.

A TROPICAL STORM has more closed isobars and a distinct rotary circulation, with winds blowing around the storm center at 39 to 73 miles an hour.

A HURRICANE or TYPHOON has many closed isobars with strong rotary winds of 74 miles an hour or more.

SMALL-CRAFT WARNING: When a hurricane moves within a few hundred miles of the coast, advisories warn operators of small crafts to take precautions and not to venture far from shore.

GALE WARNING: When winds of 38 to 55 miles per hour are expected, a gale warning is added to the advisory message.

STORM WARNING: When winds of 55 to 74 miles per hour are expected, a storm warning is added to the advisory message. Gale and storm warnings indicate the coastal area to be affected by the warning, the time during which the warning will apply, and the expected intensity of the disturbance. When gale or storm warnings are part of a tropical cyclone advisory, they may be changed to a hurricane warning if the storm continues along the coast.

HURRICANE WATCH: If the hurricane continues its advance and threatens coastal and inland regions, a hurricane watch is added to the advisory, covering a specified area and duration. A hurricane watch means that hurricane conditions are a real possibility; it does not mean they are imminent. When a hurricane watch is issued, everyone in the area covered by the watch should listen for further advisories and be prepared to act quickly if hurricane warnings are issued.

HURRICANE WARNING: When hurricane conditions are expected within twenty-four hours, a hurricane warning is added to the advisory. Hurricane warnings identify coastal areas where winds of at least 74 miles per hour are expected to occur. A warning may also describe coastal areas where dangerously high tides or exceptionally high waves are forecast, even though winds may be less than hurricane force.

When the hurricane warning is issued, all precautions should be taken immediately. Hurricane warnings are seldom issued more than twenty-four hours in advance. If the hurricane's path is unusual or

Tornadoes, spawned by hurricanes, add to the terrors of the great storms. The funnel-shaped tornado cloud is frequently obscured by the hurricane.   NOAA

That one or more tornadoes have occurred within a hurricane is known by the nature of the damage they leave.   **NOAA**

erratic, the warnings may be issued only a few hours before the beginning of hurricane conditions. Precautionary actions should begin as soon as a hurricane warning is announced.

Tornadoes sometimes develop in hurricanes and add to the terrors of the great storms. A tornado can pick up a house as if it were a toy and the vacuum in the tornado's funnel-shaped cloud can cause the house to explode. Tornadoes can carry people hundreds of yards through the air. Fortunately the paths of these whirlwinds are narrow, usually not more than a quarter of a mile. The funnel-shaped tornado cloud cannot be easily seen during a hurricane but the fact that one or more tornadoes have occurred within a hurricane is known from the type of damage they leave.

Lists of Names Used for Hurricanes

Ten-year list of names for Atlantic, Caribbean and Gulf of Mexico Tropical Storms.

1971—Arlene, Beth, Chloe, Dora, Edith, Fern, Ginger, Heidi, Irene, Janice, Kristy, Laura, Margo, Nona, Orchid, Portia, Rachel, Sandra, Terese, Verna, Wallis

1972—Agnes, Betty, Carrie, Dawn, Edna, Felice, Gerda, Harriet, Ilene, Jane, Kara, Lucile, Mae, Nadine, Odette, Polly, Rita, Sarah, Tina, Velma, Wendy

1973—Alice, Brenda, Christine, Delia, Ellen, Fran, Gilda, Helen, Imogene, Joy, Kate, Loretta, Madge, Nancy, Ona, Patsy, Rose, Sally, Tam, Vera, Wilda

1974—Alma, Becky, Carmen, Dolly, Elaine, Fifi, Gertrude, Hester, Ivy, Justine, Kathy, Linda, Marsha, Nelly, Olga, Pearl, Roxanne, Sabrina, Thelma, Viola, Wilma

1975—Amy, Blanche, Caroline, Doris, Eloise, Faye, Gladys, Hallie, Ingrid, Julia, Kitty, Lilly, Mabel, Niki, Opal, Peggy, Ruby, Sheila, Tilda, Vicky, Winnie

1976—Anna, Belle, Candice, Dottie, Emmy, Frances, Gloria, Holly, Inga, Jill, Kay, Lilias, Maria, Nola, Orpha, Pamela, Ruth, Shirley, Trixie, Vilda, Wynne

1977—Anita, Babe, Clara, Dorothy, Evelyn, Frieda, Grace, Hannah, Ida, Jodie, Kristina, Lois, Mary, Nora, Odel, Penny, Raquel, Sophia, Trudy, Virginia, Willene

1978—Amelia, Bess, Cora, Debra, Ella, Flossie, Greta, Hope, Irma, Juliet, Kendra, Louise, Martha, Noreen, Ora, Paula, Rosalie, Susan, Tanya, Vanessa, Wanda

1979—Angie, Barbara, Cindy, Dot, Eve, Franny, Gwyn, Hedda, Iris, Judy, Karen, Lana, Molly, Nita, Ophelia, Patty, Roberta, Sherry, Tess, Vesta, Wenda

1980—Abby, Bertha, Candy, Dinah, Elsie, Felicia, Georgia, Hedy, Isabel, June, Kim, Lucy, Millie, Nina, Olive, Phyllis, Rosie, Suzy, Theda, Violet, Willette

For Eastern North Pacific Tropical Storms there are only the following four sets of names. The sets are recycled after four years.

1971—Agatha, Bridget, Carlotta, Denise, Eleanor, Francene, Georgette, Hilary, Ilsa, Jewel, Katrina, Lily, Monica, Nanette, Olivia, Priscilla, Ramona, Sharon, Terry, Veronica, Winifred

1972—Annette, Bonny, Celeste, Diana, Estelle, Fernanda, Gwen, Hyacinth, Iva, Joanne, Kathleen, Liza, Madeline, Naomi, Orla, Pauline, Rebecca, Simone, Tara, Valerie, Willa

1973—Ava, Bernice, Claudia, Doreen, Emily, Florence, Glenda, Heather, Irah, Jennifer, Katherine, Lillian, Mona, Natalie, Odessa, Prudence, Roslyn, Sylvia, Tillie, Victoria, Wallie

1974—Adele, Blanca, Connie, Dolores, Eileen, Francesca, Gretchen, Helga, Ione, Joyce, Kirsten, Lorraine, Maggie, Norma, Orlene, Patricia, Rosalie, Selma, Toni, Vivian, Winona

For Central and Western North Pacific Typhoons the following names are used. Instead of starting a new set each year, the names are used consecutively.

Agnes, Bess, Carmen, Della, Elaine, Faye, Gloria, Hester, Irma, Judy, Kit, Lola, Mamie, Nina, Ora, Phyllis, Rita, Susan, Tess, Viola, Winnie

Alice, Betty, Cora, Doris, Elsie, Flossie, Grace, Helen, Ida, June, Kathy, Lorna, Marie, Nancy, Olga, Pamela, Ruby, Sally, Tilda, Violet, Wilda

Anita, Billie, Clara, Dot, Ellen, Fran, Georgia, Hope, Iris, Joan, Kate, Louise, Marge, Nora, Opal, Patsy, Ruth, Sarah, Thelma, Vera, Wanda

Amy, Babe, Carla, Dinah, Emma, Freda, Gilda, Harriet, Ivy, Jean, Kim, Lucy, Mary, Nadine, Olive, Polly, Rose, Shirley, Trix, Virginia, Wendy

Index

Page numbers in italics refer to illustrations